THE BILL OF RIGHTS

Asking Tough Questions

by Jennifer Kaul

Consultant
Tim Solie
Adjunct Professor of History
Minnesota State University, Mankato
Mankato, Minnesota

CAPSTONE PRESS
a capstone imprint

Capstone Captivate is published by Capstone Press, an imprint of Capstone.
1710 Roe Crest Drive
North Mankato, Minnesota 56003
www.capstonepub.com

Library of Congress Cataloging-in-Publication Data is available on the Library of Congress website.
ISBN: 978-1-4966-8467-7 (library binding)
ISBN: 978-1-4966-8813-2 (paperback)
ISBN: 978-1-4966-8487-5 (eBook PDF)

Summary: What are the U.S. Constitution and the Bill of Rights? Why are these documents important to America's history, and how do they affect our lives today? These questions and others are examined to inspire critical thinking for young readers.

Editorial Credits
Editor: Aaron Sautter; Designer: Sara Radka; Media Researcher: Eric Gohl; Production Specialist: Spencer Rosio

Image Credits
Alamy: Everett Collection Inc, 31; Bridgeman Images: Wood Ronsaville Harlin, Inc. USA, 20; Getty Images: Michael Latil, 33 (top); iStockphoto: adamkaz, 41, diane39, 43; Library of Congress: 40 (all); New York Public Library: 15 (bottom), 30; Newscom: Picture History, 29, UPI/Pat Benic, 45, World History Archive, 22; North Wind Picture Archives: 5, 8, 10, 11, 12, 16, 23, 36; Pixabay: Clker-Free-Vector-Images, 26 (Senate/House), GDJ, 26 (scale), MIH83, background (throughout), OpenClipart-Vectors, 26 (person); Shutterstock: chrupka, 6, Everett Historical, 15 (top), Rena Schild, 39, Strejman, 26 (top buildings), Todd Taulman Photography, 24–25, ZouZou, cover (front); Wikimedia: Public Domain, cover (back), 19, 28 (all), 33 (bottom)

Printed in the United States
PA117

Table of Contents

Words in **bold** are in the glossary.

Did the U.S. Constitution Need a Bill of Rights?

Did the U.S. **Constitution** need a Bill of Rights? What is a constitution anyway? Why did the United States need one? What exactly is a bill of rights? To better understand this, let's take a trip back in time.

HOW DID THE UNITED STATES GET STARTED?

Let's head back to the 1600s. America wasn't always like it is today. For a long time, the Native nations were the only people in North America. That changed when Europeans sailed across the Atlantic Ocean. Great Britain created 13 **colonies** that would later become the country we know today.

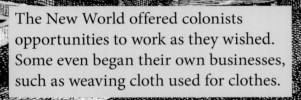

The New World offered colonists opportunities to work as they wished. Some even began their own businesses, such as weaving cloth used for clothes.

WHAT DID COLONISTS LIKE ABOUT LIVING IN AMERICA?

British colonists faced a lot of hardship and uncertainty during the 1600s and 1700s. But it was also an inspiring time. Settlers could choose where they wanted to live. They could choose to be farmers or start a business. People could follow their own religious beliefs and worship as they wished. Many people didn't have these freedoms back in Europe.

WHAT DID COLONISTS DISLIKE ABOUT LIVING IN AMERICA?

People had more opportunities in the New World. But Great Britain still owned and controlled the colonies. The colonists didn't like unfair British laws and taxes. Eventually, the colonies fought a war to win their independence from Great Britain. They became the United States of America.

United States, 1783

WHAT DID AMERICANS DISAGREE ABOUT AFTER GAINING INDEPENDENCE?

Most Americans were happy to be free of British rule. However, they disagreed about how their government should work. Some thought America needed a strong central government. Others wanted the states to have more power. Many wanted a bill of rights. They wanted a set of laws that would protect people's rights and freedoms.

But how did the colonies join together to form a new country? What inspired them to create the government that is still used today? And why did people feel that the Bill of Rights had to be added to the Constitution right away?

Important Events in Building America

1773: Boston Tea Party; colonists in Massachusetts dump tea into Boston harbor to **protest** Tea Act

1774: Great Britain passes several unfair laws that become known as the Intolerable Acts

1776: The 13 colonies sign the Declaration of Independence

1777: Articles of Confederation are created

1783: Treaty of Paris is signed by United States and Great Britain; the Revolutionary War ends

1787: U.S. Constitution is created

1791: The Bill of Rights is added to the Constitution

CHAPTER 1

Why Did the Colonists Fight the Revolutionary War?

By the 1760s the colonists had grown tired of British troops occupying their towns and cities.

WHAT WAS THE RELATIONSHIP BETWEEN THE COLONIES AND GREAT BRITAIN?

In 1700 about 250,000 colonists lived in America. By the 1760s, more than 2 million people lived there. People thought of themselves as Americans, rather than British colonists. But the colonies still belonged to Great Britain. The British government ruled over everything, and people had to follow British law. This led to several conflicts between the colonists and the British.

The British often sent troops to the colonies to defend them from French and Spanish forces. The British didn't ask the colonists if they wanted these troops. But they did expect Americans to pay for them.

England also created many unfair taxes to help pay for wars in Europe. The British taxed many goods like glass, paint, paper, and tea. These taxes made it hard for colonists to sell things.

FACT

John Adams wrote about the colonists views of unfair British laws in his diary. He said, "The People . . . have become more attentive to their Liberties . . ." They were "more inquisitive" about their rights. And they were "more determined to defend them . . ."

WHAT WAS TAXATION WITHOUT REPRESENTATION?

The colonists were angry about the British taxes. They called it "taxation without representation." This meant they were being taxed by Britain's government but had no say in it. Many colonists protested. Others stopped buying British goods.

During the Boston Tea Party colonists disguised themselves as Native people. They didn't want to be recognized. They also wanted to show how they thought of themselves as free Americans, rather than British citizens.

One form of protest was the Boston Tea Party. Tea was a favorite drink in the colonies. But England passed an unfair tax on tea. In 1773 a group of colonists boarded a ship at the harbor in Boston, Massachusetts. They dumped thousands of pounds of tea into the harbor to protest the tax. The tea company and the British government were angry. To punish the colonists, England passed several harsher laws.

The Intolerable Acts allowed British soldiers to search colonists' homes and take their possessions without permission.

WHAT WERE THE INTOLERABLE ACTS?

The colonists called the new laws the Intolerable Acts. These acts assigned British governors to rule over the colonies. They forced colonists to feed and house British soldiers. They even protected British officials from being punished when they broke the law.

Colonists could not hold town meetings without permission. British authorities could search colonists' homes without a good reason. And British officials also tried to take the colonists' guns. Soon, the colonists had endured enough. Many were ready to fight for their rights.

DID ALL OF THE COLONISTS AGREE TO FIGHT THE BRITISH?

Many colonists were eager to fight for independence. But some didn't want to fight a war. They felt that Great Britain was their homeland. They depended on it for trade, government, and protection.

The colonists were soon divided. Those who wanted to separate from Britain called themselves patriots. Those who wanted to remain with England were called loyalists. The remaining colonists stayed neutral.

Loyalists were often mocked and forced to leave their home towns by colonists who wanted to end British rule.

The Revolutionary War finally broke out in 1775. But the colonists often argued amongst themselves. Most loyalists were wealthy. They lived comfortably and weren't harmed by the British taxes. But many worried that the war would change their situation. Some loyalists even joined British troops and fought against the patriots. The patriots fought back by mocking the loyalists and destroying their property. The disagreements between the two groups would continue even after the war.

WHAT WOULD HAPPEN NEXT?

By 1783 the colonists had won the war and gained their independence. But now they were on their own. The country's leaders needed to create a new government. But what did they want it to look like? How did they want their new country to work?

What was the Declaration of Independence?

The Declaration of Independence said that the thirteen colonies wanted to be a separate country from Great Britain. It said, "We hold these truths to be self-evident, that all men are created equal, that they are endowed by their Creator with certain unalienable Rights, that among these are Life, Liberty and the pursuit of Happiness." The Declaration was approved by the Continental Congress on July 4th, 1776.

CHAPTER 2

What Were the Articles of Confederation?

After declaring their independence, the colonies' leaders knew they'd need to form a new government. The Continental Congress created America's first constitution in 1777. It was called the **Articles of Confederation**. By themselves, the states were limited in what they could do. The nation's leaders knew that a central government was important. The Articles would help bring the states together and work together as one nation.

However, the writers of the Articles were careful not to give Congress too much power. They worried that a large central government couldn't serve all of the people well. Plus, the colonies were already fighting a war against a powerful government. They didn't want to have to do it again. So the Articles were written to give most of the power to the states.

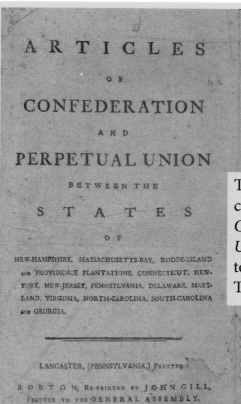

The full title of America's first constitution was *Articles of Confederation and Perpetual Union*. It was the first document to name the new country The United States of America.

How Do State Governments Work?

Each state follows its own constitution. Many of these include a Declaration of Rights to protect the rights of the people. America's Bill of Rights was based on the rights listed in the Virginia state constitution. They were written by a man named George Mason. Mason is now known as the "Father of the Bill of Rights."

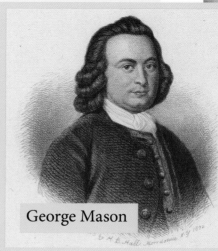

George Mason

From 1786 to 1787, Revolutionary War veteran Daniel Shays led an uprising to try to overthrow the government in Massachusetts. The U.S. government was unable to help stop the uprising. Shays' Rebellion helped show the need for a strong central government.

WHAT POWERS DID THE ARTICLES GIVE THE STATES?

Under the Articles, the U.S. Congress was in charge of things that affected all states. These included war, money, and mail. But each state could choose whether or not to pay taxes to the U.S. government. States could also refuse to provide soldiers to support the country. Many chose not to.

Congress was not allowed to take action or pass laws that affected the country without permission. To pass a national law, nine states had to agree to it. All of the states needed to agree to add **amendments** to the Articles. But states often disagreed on how to handle different issues. It was difficult for Congress to get anything done. The government didn't run very well and the country was weaker as a result.

It soon became clear that the Articles weren't a long-term solution. The U.S. needed a more powerful central government.

CHAPTER 3

How Was the U.S. Constitution Created?

A Constitutional Convention was called in 1787. A group of 55 **delegates** from the states met in Philadelphia, Pennsylvania. At first, they planned to fix the Articles of Confederation. But it soon became clear that they'd need to get rid of the Articles and start over.

Constitutional Convention Leaders

1. George Washington, Virginia
- commander in chief of Continental Army during Revolutionary War
- served as president of Constitutional Convention
- became the first president of the United States of America

2. Benjamin Franklin, Pennsylvania
- wrote the Albany Plan that led to Articles of Confederation
- helped write the Declaration of Independence and the Treaty of Paris
- at 81 years old, was the oldest delegate of the Convention

FACT
The Convention representatives met in secret in what is now called Independence Hall. This was so delegates could speak honestly and without the pressure of other colonists.

3. James Madison, Virginia
- wrote the first draft of the U.S. Constitution
- wrote the Bill of Rights
- became fourth president of the United States

4. Alexander Hamilton, New York
- fought in the Revolutionary War
- delegate of Constitutional Convention
- became first Secretary of Treasury

WHAT WAS DEBATED AT THE CONVENTION?

There were many disagreements at the Convention. Some delegates argued that the country should have a strong central government. But others worried that this would threaten the states' rights. They wanted the states to be free to make their own laws.

Delegates at the Constitutional Convention often argued about how the new government should work.

The delegates all agreed that the states should have a fair voice in the government. But they disagreed on how many representatives the states should have. Some thought each state should have the same number of representatives. This would guarantee that states had an equal say in laws passed by the government. But others felt that states with a lot of people should have a greater voice. They thought the number of representatives should be based on a state's population. This would give more of the people a voice in the government.

The delegates debated the issue for a long time. But they struggled to find a solution that treated each state fairly. Finally, Oliver Ellsworth and Roger Sherman, delegates from Connecticut, came up with a way to end the disagreement.

FACT

The delegates at the Convention also argued about enslaved people. Some wanted enslaved people to count toward a state's population. This would also give the states more representatives in Congress. But others thought of enslaved people as property. They didn't think enslaved people should be included.

WHAT WAS DECIDED?

Ellsworth and Sherman knew states were concerned about having a fair voice in government. States with many people wanted several representatives. This would give them more votes in decisions that affected the entire country. But states with fewer people wanted the states to all have an equal number of representatives. They felt that more representatives would give states too much power to pass laws they didn't like.

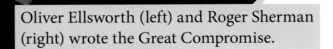

Oliver Ellsworth (left) and Roger Sherman (right) wrote the Great Compromise.

The two men worked out a plan called the Great Compromise. Some representatives would be based on a state's population. Some would be equal for each state. Three-fifths of a state's enslaved people would be counted. The states agreed to this idea.

The Compromise led to the formation of the U.S. House of Representatives and the U.S. Senate. The number of representatives in the House is based on each state's population. The Senate has two senators from each state.

What Did the Delegates Decide About Slavery?

The delegates argued a lot about the practice of slavery. Many from the northern states thought slavery should be **abolished**. But in the South, enslaved black people provided the hard labor needed on farms and plantations. Many Southerners wanted slavery to continue.

The delegates decided to let the slave trade continue until 1808. Samuel Hopkins was outraged. He said, "How does it appear . . . that these States, who have been fighting for liberty . . . enslave their fellow men . . ."

WHAT HAPPENED NEXT?

After agreeing on how to form the government, the delegates wrote the U.S. Constitution. Thirty-nine of them signed it. It was then sent to the 13 states to be **ratified**. Each state held its own convention to discuss the Constitution. Finally, they voted on whether or not to accept it.

FACT

George Washington was the first to sign the Constitution. He signed it on September 17, 1787.

?

WHAT DOES THE PREAMBLE SAY?

The Constitution begins with the Preamble. It starts, "We the people of the United States, . . ." This shows that the Constitution was written by American **citizens**. Next it says, ". . . in Order to form a more perfect union . . ." This shows that the Constitution was created to help make the country better.

The Preamble says that the Constitution would give justice and **tranquility** to the people. It also promises to provide a common defense for the country. The delegates hoped the Constitution would allow U.S. citizens to be happy, healthy, and free. It was their hope for their own time and for all future Americans.

WHAT ARE THE ARTICLES OF THE CONSTITUTION?

The rest of the Constitution contains seven sections, or articles. Articles I, II, and III create the three branches of government. Each branch keeps the others from having too much power.

Three Branches of U.S. Government

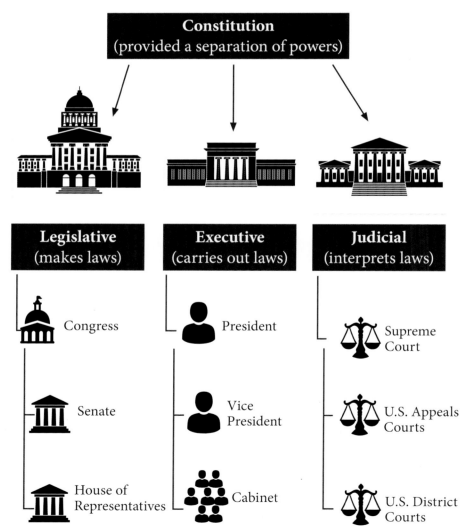

Constitution
(provided a separation of powers)

Legislative (makes laws)	Executive (carries out laws)	Judicial (interprets laws)
Congress	President	Supreme Court
Senate	Vice President	U.S. Appeals Courts
House of Representatives	Cabinet	U.S. District Courts

Article I describes the **legislative branch**. It is made of the House of Representatives and the Senate. Together, these form the United States Congress. The Congress creates bills that become laws for the country.

Article II creates the **executive branch**. This is the president. The president's job is to sign bills into laws, enforce the laws, and command the military.

Article III forms the **judicial branch**. This includes the country's courts and the Supreme Court. Its job is to interpret the law and use it to make decisions in court cases.

The rest of the articles tell more about how the government works. They describe how states should treat each other. They explain how the Constitution can be amended, or changed. And they state that the Constitution will be "the supreme Law of the Land."

FACT

The Convention delegates are known as the framers of the Constitution. They are also called the Founding Fathers.

HOW DID AMERICANS REACT TO THE CONSTITUTION?

People had different thoughts about the new Constitution. One group was the Federalists. They supported the Constitution and tried to convince the states to approve it. The other group was the Anti-Federalists. They opposed the Constitution. They didn't want the states to accept it.

WHY DID THE FEDERALISTS SUPPORT THE CONSTITUTION?

Federalists supported the Constitution because they felt it would fix problems created by the Articles of Confederation. Alexander Hamilton, James Madison, and John Jay were Federalists. They wrote 85 essays called the *Federalist Papers*. These papers argued that a strong central government was important for the country.

Alexander Hamilton

James Madison

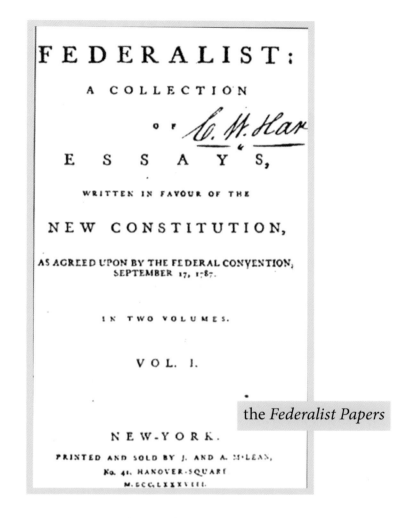

the *Federalist Papers*

One strong point that John Jay made was that a national government could better defend the country in times of war. Alexander Hamilton believed a central government would help keep peace between the states. James Madison agreed that the Constitution gave some central powers to the national government. But he argued that the states would still control their own governments and do what they thought was best for the people.

WHY DID THE ANTI-FEDERALISTS OPPOSE THE CONSTITUTION?

The Anti-Federalists believed the Constitution gave the national government too much power. Patrick Henry was an Anti-Federalist. He feared that the Constitution would lead to the country being run by the rich. He didn't want the needs of other citizens to be forgotten or ignored.

Patrick Henry feared that a strong central government would lead to corruption. His arguments in the Anti-Federalist papers helped pave the way for the Bill of Rights.

Alarm ! Alarm ! Alarm !

A fcheme has been difcovered. The Federalifts are raifing *money* ; they are hiring men to go through the whole city in fearch of electors to gain their votes, they are fending their lawyers in every direction and in every corner, on horfeback and on foot, in the city and in the fuburbs. They have fworn to leave no ftone unturned, and from fuch extraordinary and un-paralleled exertions, they ftill calculate on gaining the victory. Their leading men have fpent the night in clofe divan. What new plot will be the confequence, time only can develope. Re-publicans! meet them on their own ground! difperfe yourfelves through the wards, and bring up all your votes; fo fhall you ftill triumph, and this final act of defperation fhall only tend to exhibit the laft agonizing ftruggles of a deteftable expiring fac-t.on.

WAYNE.

Anti-Federalists sometimes published leaflets accusing Federalists of tampering with elections.

Many Anti-Federalists also wanted the states to stay separate. They didn't want the states to be combined into one country. They feared that the states and their citizens would lose their rights. Many Americans felt that the Constitution needed a bill of rights that would guarantee basic rights for everyone.

Anti-Federalists wrote papers too. These papers predicted bad outcomes for America if it adopted the Constitution. Some Federalists began to worry. They thought the states would vote against the Constitution if it didn't include a bill of rights.

CHAPTER 4

What Is the Bill of Rights?

Many Federalists didn't think a bill of rights was needed. Some felt that the states' constitutions already protected people's rights. Others argued that the Constitution already covered most rights of the people.

Eventually, the states agreed to the Constitution, but only if it included certain rights. James Madison wrote nineteen amendments to the Constitution in 1789. Many were based on George Mason's Declaration of Rights in Virginia's state constitution. Madison wanted to make sure people's rights were protected. Thomas Jefferson agreed that "a bill of rights is what the people are entitled to against every government on earth."

Twelve of the amendments were agreed to by Congress. Ten were ratified by the states in 1791. They became known as the Bill of Rights.

The U.S. Congress made several revisions to James Madison's amendments before sending them to the States to be ratified.

RESOLVED, BY THE SENATE AND HOUSE OF REPRESENTATIVES OF THE UNITED STATES OF AMERICA IN CONGRESS ASSEMBLED, two thirds of both Houses concurring, That the following Articles be proposed to the Legislatures of the several States, as Amendments to the Constitution of the United States, all or any of which Articles, when ratified by three fourths of the said Legislatures, to be valid to all intents and purposes as part of the said Constitution—Viz.

ARTICLES in addition to, and amendment of, the Constitution of the United States of America, proposed by Congress, and ratified by the Legislatures of the several States, pursuant to the fifth Article of the original Constitution.

ARTICLE THE FIRST.

After the first enumeration, required by the first Article of the Constitution, there shall be one Representative for every thirty thousand, until the number shall amount to one hundred, after which the proportion shall be so regulated by Congress, that there shall be not less than one hundred Representatives, nor less than one Representative for every forty thousand persons, until the number of Representatives shall amount to two hundred, after which the proportion shall be so regulated by Congress, that there shall not be less than two hundred Representatives, nor less than one Representative for every fifty thousand persons.

ARTICLE THE SECOND.

No law varying the compensation to the members of Congress, shall take effect, until an election of Representatives shall have intervened.

ARTICLE THE THIRD.

Congress shall make no law establishing religion or prohibiting the free exercise thereof, nor shall the rights of Conscience be infringed.

ARTICLE THE FOURTH.

The Freedom of Speech, and of the Press, and the right of the People peaceably to assemble, and to apply to the Government for a redress of grievances, shall not be infringed.

What Was the Magna Carta?

The Magna Carta is a set of rights agreed to by King John of England in 1215. It promised to protect certain rights and provide justice for several British nobles. The American colonists wanted these rights too. The Bill of Rights was inspired in part by the Magna Carta.

WHAT DOES THE BILL OF RIGHTS SAY?

The Bill of Rights includes the first 10 amendments to the U.S. Constitution. It guarantees certain rights for all citizens.

- The First Amendment protects people's freedom of religion and speech. People have the right to worship and say what they think without being punished by the government. People can also meet peacefully to criticize their government.

- The Second Amendment gives people the right to own and use guns as long as they follow the law.

- The Third Amendment says that people can't be forced to let soldiers live in their homes during times of peace.

- The Fourth Amendment says that people's homes can't be searched without a good reason.

- The Fifth through Eighth Amendments protect people's right to fair treatment and a fair trial if they're accused of a crime.

- The Ninth and Tenth Amendments state that all other rights not covered by the Constitution are given to the people.

The Bill of Rights
Ratified December 15, 1791

Article I
Congress shall make no law respecting an establishment of religion, or prohibiting the free exercise thereof; or abridging the freedom of speech, or of the press; or the right of the people peaceably to assemble, and to petition the Government for a redress of grievances.

Article II
A well regulated Militia, being necessary to the security of a free State, the right of the people to keep and bear Arms, shall not be infringed.

Article III
No Soldier shall, in time of peace be quartered in any house, without the consent of the Owner, nor in time of war, but in a manner to be prescribed by law.

Article IV
The right of the people to be secure in their persons, houses, papers, and effects, against unreasonable searches and seizures, shall not be violated, and no Warrants shall issue, but upon probable cause, supported by Oath or affirmation, and particularly describing the place to be searched, and the persons or things to be seized.

Article V
No person shall be held to answer for a capital, or otherwise infamous crime, unless on a presentment or indictment of a Grand Jury, except in cases arising in the land or naval forces, or in the Militia, when in actual service in time of War or public danger; nor shall any person be subject for the same offence to be twice put in jeopardy of life or limb; nor shall be compelled in any criminal case to be a witness against himself, nor be deprived of life, liberty, or property, without due process of law; nor shall private property be taken for public use, without just compensation.

Article VI
In all criminal prosecutions, the accused shall enjoy the right to a speedy and public trial, by an impartial jury of the State and district wherein the crime shall have been committed, which district shall have been previously ascertained by law, and to be informed of the nature and cause of the accusation; to be confronted with the witnesses against him; to have compulsory process for obtaining witnesses in his favor, and to have the Assistance of Counsel for his defence.

Article VII
In suits at common law, where the value in controversy shall exceed twenty dollars, the right of trial by jury shall be preserved, and no fact tried by a jury, shall be otherwise re-examined in any Court of the United States, than according to the rules of the common law.

Article VIII
Excessive bail shall not be required, nor excessive fines imposed, nor cruel and unusual punishments inflicted.

Article IX
The enumeration in the Constitution, of certain rights, shall not be construed to deny or disparage others retained by the people.

Article X
The powers not delegated to the United States by the Constitution, nor prohibited by it to the States, are reserved to the States respectively, or to the people.

In July 1788, parades in several cities celebrated ratification of the new U.S. Constitution. The parade in New York featured the federal ship *Hamilton*, which was pulled by a team of horses.

WHY WAS THE BILL OF RIGHTS IMPORTANT?

Many of the freedoms granted by the Bill of Rights can be traced back to the colonists' struggles with England. Many colonists left Great Britain to seek religious freedom. The Bill of Rights makes sure the people's right to worship freely can't be taken away.

Before and during the Revolutionary War, England tried to stop colonists from owning guns. They didn't want the colonies to be able to fight. The Bill of Rights allows Americans to own guns to protect themselves and to fight in times of war.

The colonists felt it was unfair to be forced to let British soldiers live in their homes. They didn't like having their homes searched without evidence of a crime. They also didn't like unfair trials in the courts. Americans wanted all of their rights to be protected by law. The Constitution and the Bill of Rights protect these rights for all U.S. citizens. They cannot be taken away by the government.

CHAPTER 5

How Does the Bill of Rights Affect Americans Today?

The Constitution is still the foundation of America's government. It tells the nation's leaders how the country should be run. It keeps any one person from having too much power. It protects the rights of the states and U.S. citizens. The Constitution is followed closely in court cases. Judges use it to make sure people's rights are respected by other people and the government.

DO PEOPLE STILL BELIEVE IN THE BILL OF RIGHTS?

People today often have different views of the Bill of Rights. Some people disagree about how much freedom it provides. For example, some people feel there should be restrictions on who can own guns. But others strongly feel that this right should not be limited.

The Bill of Rights protects the right of people to gather and speak out about important issues, such as Climate Change.

There are similar arguments about freedom of religion and speech. Should people be free to do and say things that are insulting to others? If so, how much should be allowed? These disagreements have taken place for as long as the Bill of Rights has existed. People will likely continue to disagree far into the future.

WHAT OTHER CHANGES HAVE BEEN MADE TO THE CONSTITUTION?

America's founders knew that no government is perfect. They realized that more changes would need to be made beyond the Bill of Rights. The Constitution is still the foundation of U.S. government, but it has gone through many changes over time.

The 13th–15th Amendments stopped slavery in the United States and gave black men the right to vote.

Elizabeth Cady Stanton (left) and Susan B. Anthony (right) believed that women deserved the right to vote. They worked for many years to get the 19th Amendment passed.

There have been 27 amendments to the Constitution, including the Bill of Rights. Some amendments made slavery illegal in America and guaranteed rights to all people. Others gave the right to vote to women and people ages

The 26th Amendment allows people 18 and older to vote in elections.

18 and up. Still others provide rules for electing the president, vice president, and senators. There are even amendments that state how long a president can serve in office.

Major Constitutional Amendments

1791 – Amendments 1-10: The Bill of Rights

1865 – Amendment 13: Ended slavery in the United States

1868 – Amendment 14: Made all people born in the country U.S. citizens

1870 – Amendment 15: Gave men of all races the right to vote, including formerly enslaved people

1920 – Amendment 19: Gave women the right to vote

1971 – Amendment 26: Gave U.S. citizens 18 years old and older the right to vote

HOW WOULD THE UNITED STATES BE DIFFERENT WITHOUT THE BILL OF RIGHTS?

Think about life in America today. The Bill of Rights and other amendments give people the freedom to live as they please. To better understand these freedoms, it's important to look back in time and think about how the United States has changed.

Imagine that you had lived in the late 1700s when America was becoming a country. What would your thoughts have been about the Constitution and the Bill of Rights? At the time, many people thought the Bill of Rights wasn't necessary. Would you have supported the idea of a strong central government? Or do you think that the Bill of Rights was needed to guarantee certain freedoms for people?

Large crowds of U.S. citizens often gather in Washington, D.C. The First Amendment gives people the right to gather and speak out about issues that are important to them.

What would America look like today if the colonies hadn't broken free from British rule? How would the country be different if the Articles of Confederation had succeeded? Did America really need the Constitution and the Bill of Rights? How different would life in America be today without these important documents?

More Questions About the Bill of Rights

What happened to the original Bill of Rights document?

The Bill of Rights is located in the Rotunda at the National Archives Museum in Washington, D.C. This is also where the Constitution and the Declaration of Independence are displayed. The Rotunda is kept cool and dark to help preserve these historic documents.

How is an amendment added to the Constitution?

Many things need to happen to add an amendment to the Constitution. First, Congress must propose an amendment. Then two-thirds of both the House of Representatives and the Senate must agree to add the amendment. A constitutional convention may also propose an amendment.

After Congress approves an amendment, it goes to the states. The government in each state votes on whether or not to ratify the amendment. The amendment is added to the Constitution once it has been ratified by three-fourths of the states.

Do other countries have a constitution or a bill of rights?

Several countries have constitutions, but few are as old as the U.S. Constitution. There are over 900 constitutions in the world. Around ten new constitutions are written each year.

Many countries have a bill of rights or something similar. For example, the Canadian Charter of Rights and Freedoms was established in 1982. It includes rights like those in the U.S. Bill of Rights. Everyone is considered equal by law.

The U.S. Constitution is displayed in the Rotunda at the National Archives Museum in Washington, D.C.

GLOSSARY

abolish (uh-BOL-ish)—to officially put an end to something

amendment (uh-MEND-muhnt)—a change made to a law or a legal document

Articles of Confederation (AR-ti-kuhls UHV kuhn-fed-er-AY-shuhn)—the first constitution of the United States that governed the country during the Revolutionary War

citizen (SI-tuh-zuhn)—a member of a country or state who has the right to live there

colonies (KAH-luh-nees)—the 13 British territories that became the United States of America

constitution (kahn-stuh-TOO-shuhn)—the system of laws in a country or state that describe the rights of the people and the powers of the government

delegate (DEL-uh-guht)—a person chosen to represent a group of people at a meeting or event

executive branch (ig-ZE-kyoo-tiv BRANCH)—the part of government that enforces laws, commands the military, and interacts with foreign governments

judicial branch (joo-DISH-uhl BRANCH)—the part of government that explains and interprets laws

legislative branch (LEJ-iss-lay-tiv BRANCH)—the part of government that passes bills to create laws

protest (pro-TEST)—to object to something strongly and publicly

ratify (RAT-uh-fy)—to formally agree to or officially approve a document

tranquility (trang-KWIL-i-tee)—a state of calmness and peace

READ MORE

Demuth, Patricia Brennan. *What is the Constitution?* New York: Penguin Workshop, 2018.

Donohue, Moira Rose. *The U.S. Constitution: Why It Matters to You.* New York: Children's Press, 2020.

Leavitt, Amie Jane. *The Bill of Rights in Translation: What It Really Means.* North Mankato, MN: Capstone Press, 2018.

INTERNET SITES

Interactive Constitution
https://constitutioncenter.org/interactive-constitution

Know Your Rights
https://www.factmonster.com/us/laws-and-rights/know-your-rights

U.S. Constitution
https://www.brainpop.com/socialstudies/ushistory/usconstitution/

INDEX